VR ON THE JOB
Understanding Virtual
and Augmented Reality

USING VR IN THE MILITARY

Jeri Freedman

Cavendish
Square

New York

Published in 2020 by Cavendish Square Publishing, LLC
243 5th Avenue, Suite 136, New York, NY 10016

Cataloging-in-Publication Data

Names: Freedman, Jeri.
Title: VR in the military / Jeri Freedman.
Description: New York : Cavendish Square Publishing, 2020. | Series: VR on the job: understanding virtual and augmented reality | Includes glossary and index.
Identifiers: ISBN 9781502645722 (pbk.) | ISBN 9781502645739 (library bound) | ISBN 9781502645746 (ebook)
Subjects: LCSH: United States--Armed Forces--Vocational guidance--Juvenile literature. | Virtual reality in electronic games--Juvenile literature. | Augmented reality--Juvenile literature.
Classification: LCC UB147.F74 2020 | DDC 355.0023/73--dc23

Editorial Director: David McNamara
Editor: Chet'la Sebree
Copy Editor: Nathan Heidelberger
Associate Art Director: Alan Sliwinski
Designer: Christina Shults
Production Coordinator: Karol Szymczuk
Photo Research: J8 Media

The photographs in this book are used by permission and through the courtesy of: Cover Sean Prior/Alamy Stock Photo; p. 3 (and used throughout the book) Click Bestsellers/Shutterstock.com; p. 4 Claudio Arnese/iStock/Getty Images; p. 7 US Army Photo/Alamy Stock Photo; p. 10-11 Georgijevic/iStock/Getty Images; p. 13 Mirrorpix/Getty Images; p. 14 Morton Heilig/Wikimedia Commons/ File:Sensorama morton heilig patent.png/Public Domain; p. 16 Rina Castelnuovo/ Bloomberg/Getty Images; p. 19 Arterra/UIG/Getty Images; p. 21 US Army photo; p. 23 Ian Waldie/ Getty Images; p. 25 LightField Studios/Shutterstock.com; p. 27 U.S. Navy photo by John F. Williams/ Wikimedia Commons/ File:US Navy 100914N7676W065 Clarke Lethin, explains to Dr. Walter F. Jones, left, and George Solhanhow a virtual puppeteer interacts with Marines.jpg/Public Domain; p. 30 U.S. Air Force photo by Tech. Sgt. Darnell T. Cannady; p. 35 U.S. Marine Corps photo by Lance Cpl. Shane T. Manson; p. 38 DoD Photo by U.S. Army Sgt. James K. McCann; p. 41 U.S. Air Force photo by J.M. Eddins Jr.; p. 43 U.S. Air Force photo/Airman 1st Class Alyssa M. Akers; p. 440 Robert Daemmrich Photography Inc/Corbis/Getty Images; p. 46 Monkey Business Images/Shutterstock.com; p. 48-49 Jacob Lund/Shutterstock.com; p. 54 Gorodenkoff/Shutterstock.com; p. 58-59 Joel Carillet/iStockphoto.com; p. 60 U.S. Air Force photo by Airman 1st Class Samuel Conteras; p. 63 Markus von Luecken/Corbis/Getty Images; p. 65 Artie Medvedev/Shutterstock.com; p. 66 'Virtual Iraq' Combats Horrors of War for Troops with PTSD/DVIDS; p. 68 kudla/Shutterstock.com.

Printed in the United States of America

CONTENTS

1 VIRTUAL AND AUGMENTED REALITY

What if the first-person shooter games you play in the arcade were the basis of your future career? They just might be if you're hoping to pursue a virtual and augmented reality–related job in the military. Virtual reality (VR) digitally creates an artificial environment that a person's senses perceive as if it were real. Augmented reality (AR) overlays virtual elements on a person's view of the real world. Both of these technologies have uses in military applications. All the branches of the military have started using some form of these technologies and are exploring future applications.

Opposite: Virtual reality simulators can provide soldiers with an immersive combat experience.

CREATING A VIRTUAL WORLD

We experience the world through our senses, such as seeing and hearing. Essentially, sensors in our eyes, nose, mouth, ears, and skin send data from the environment to our brain. Our brain then processes that data into meaningful information. For example, cells in the retina in the back of our eyes transmit to the brain the wavelength, angle, and intensity of light waves that strike these cells. The brain then interprets this information to form an image. Virtual reality works by presenting our senses with computer-generated data that our brains interpret in the same way that they process real sensory data. We thus experience a virtual three-dimensional environment as if it were real. A person can move and manipulate objects within it, causing it to change. These types of experiences are often called "immersive" because a person feels as if he or she is actually surrounded by the virtual environment.

To experience the sense of virtual reality, people wear gloves and headsets that contain sensors. These sensors allow a computer system to identify where the person is looking and how his or her body is moving. In some cases, the person walks on a treadmill that creates the illusion of walking through the environment. These treadmills are omnidirectional, which means they allow movement in all directions.

To be effective, virtual reality must take into consideration how the human body works. For example, because people have peripheral vision, they see what is

Soldiers wearing virtual reality gear can undergo virtual combat training. The hardware they're wearing tracks their movements so that their virtual environments respond accordingly.

to the side of them at the same time that they see what is straight ahead. Similarly, a VR experience must account for the fact that people have a vestibular system. This system consists of components in the ears that tell a person's brain how his or her body is oriented within the environment. The brain then adjusts the muscles so the person can keep his or her balance. If a person's movement and vision within a virtual environment are not properly coordinated, the vestibular system receives confusing signals, and he or she can experience motion sickness. This is what happens to some people when they try to read in a moving car.

AUGMENTED REALITY

In contrast to virtual reality, augmented reality doesn't create the sense that a person is in a different environment. Rather, it superimposes digital information—images, sounds, or text—onto the real environment in which a person is located. Examples include the heads-up display (a transparent screen in a helmet on which data is displayed) used by Iron Man in the Marvel movies, and the Pokémon characters superimposed on real locations in the *Pokémon Go* game. Superimposition means that one image is placed over another, so both can be seen at the same time. AR can be produced on a variety of devices, including glasses, handheld computers, smartphones, head-mounted displays, and even smart contact lenses.

AR relies on technologies such as simultaneous localization and mapping (SLAM) and depth tracking—using a sensor to calculate the distance the user is from an object. In AR, cameras, sensors, and the global positioning system (GPS) in the device collect data about the location of a user and the nature and location of objects in the environment around that person. The computer in the device processes the data from the cameras and sensors and creates a 3D model of the environment. In AR-enabled devices, the digital images are projected onto the screen of the device, allowing the user to view them superimposed on the environment.

There are several different types of AR. Marker-based AR, also referred to as image recognition, shows a digital image when the camera identifies a particular object in the environment. This object is called the "marker." When the device encounters the marker, it initiates a digital animation for the user to view. Thus, a photo in a magazine might turn into a three-dimensional model when viewed through an AR device. Markerless AR, however, does not require a specific trigger. For instance, you can add digital elements like furniture to your living room without any sort of marker.

There is also location-based or position-based AR. This type of AR uses a device's GPS, a compass, a gyroscope (a device that provides directional information), and an accelerometer (a device that measures speed). These components provide the device with data about the user's location and speed of movement, which determines what information is displayed for the user. For example, during military activity, information on the upcoming terrain could be revealed to a soldier moving through an area.

In this image, augmented reality superimposes information about businesses on a user's view of the city.

EARLY VR AND AR

The first use of media to create a sense of virtual reality occurred in the late 1950s, when cinematographer Morton Heilig created the Sensorama. It was a cabinet in which a person sat to view a brief movie. It used stereo speakers, a 3D display, fans, a vibrating chair, and devices that released scents to provide an immersive experience of the film. Heilig created six short films for his device. He also invented the first head-mounted VR display in 1960. Called the Telesphere Mask, it allowed the wearer to view and hear a film but not interact with it. Viewer interaction via a head-mounted display became possible in 1961.

Two engineers, Charles Comeau and James Bryan, designed a head-mounted display called Headsight. The wearer's head movements controlled the motion of a remote camera, presenting the viewer with an image of the remote environment as if he were there. Its purpose was to let soldiers safely view remote locations in an immersive experience.

In 1965, computer scientist Ivan Sutherland wrote a paper called "The Ultimate Display" in which he described a computer-controlled device that could create a virtual world and allow people to manipulate objects in it. His paper became the model for the development of virtual reality. In 1968, Sutherland and Bob Sproull, one of his students, created Sword of Damocles. It is widely regarded as the first VR headset, as it presented different images based on where the user's head was positioned.

THE FIRST FLIGHT SIMULATOR

Inventor Edward Link developed one of the first virtual reality applications. In 1929, he created the Blue Box flight simulator, more commonly known as the Link Trainer. It was the first commercial flight simulator. He used motors to control a steering column, like that of an airplane, and a rudder (a component that pivots to provide stability to a plane in motion). As the trainee seated in a replica of a plane's cockpit manipulated the controls, the motors produced the

The Blue Box flight simulator was the earliest virtual flight system used to train military pilots.

pitch and roll that a pilot would experience in a real plane. In other words, the person experienced the up-and-down and side-to-side movements of a plane in the simulator. The trainer even had a motor-driven device that could imitate turbulence. The Link Trainer solved a problem experienced by the US military: how to safely train pilots. In 1934, the US Army Air Force bought six of these devices, making it the first virtual reality application used by the military. In World War II, the Link Trainer was used to teach more than half a million airmen.

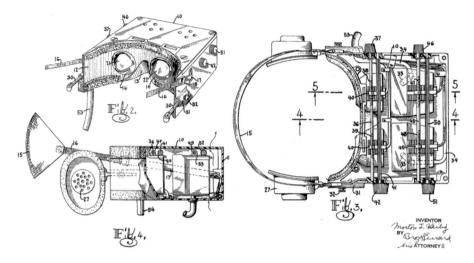

This diagram from the patent for the Sensorama shows the design of the system. The patent gave the Sensorama's creator, Morton Heilig, the exclusive right to create, use, and sell the system.

In 1975, Myron Krueger, a virtual reality computer artist, developed an "artificial reality" laboratory. He called it Videoplace. Videoplace used tools such as projectors and video cameras to allow people to interact with digital objects. Many of Videoplace's concepts were later used in virtual reality devices.

Despite all of this early technology, the term "virtual reality" wasn't coined until 1987. Jaron Lanier, a computer scientist, came up with the term. While working for Atari, a gaming company started in 1972, Lanier and Tom Zimmerman invented the Dataglove. This device collected data from a user's hand movements and transmitted it to a computer. Lanier later founded VPL Research, a company focused on commercializing virtual reality technologies. It was the first company to sell virtual reality goggles, including the EyePhone head-mounted display. As developments in virtual reality continued, augmented reality finally made its debut.

The idea of augmented reality appeared in 1990 in a paper by two Boeing Corporation scientists: Thomas Caudell and David Mizell. In 1992, Louis Rosenberg, a scientist working at the Air Force Research Lab, created one of the first augmented reality systems: Virtual Fixtures. The user wore a full upper-body exoskeleton, a device worn over the body, that transmitted information to two computer-controlled robotic arms. The system incorporated visual and audio devices that provided sensory information such as guidelines, views of terrain, and sounds to help the user guide the arms. The display superimposed the robotic arms on top of the users arms to make it easier to manipulate them.

VR AND AR IN THE TWENTY-FIRST CENTURY

Throughout the 1990s, the development of VR was fueled by the gaming industry, which developed VR hardware such as displays and gloves. In the twenty-first century, mobile computer technology and improvements in display technology and 3D graphics have made it easier to develop VR and AR applications. Components such as depth-sensing cameras, motion controllers, and better human-computer interfaces are speeding the advancement of VR and AR applications. In the military, applications are expanding far beyond training.

2 MILITARY APPLICATIONS OF VR AND AR

Technology is one of the most crucial factors in war. For instance, the use of the machine gun in World War I had a devastating impact. Therefore, when a new technology such as virtual or augmented reality becomes available, all the branches of the military are quick to explore it. Virtual and augmented reality are being used by the US Army, Navy, Marines, Coast Guard, and Air Force for a variety of reasons. These technologies are being used to train pilots to fly planes and medics to treat injuries. They are also being used to help soldiers navigate battlefield terrains, to control unmanned vehicles, to enhance boot camp, and to improve decision-making and leadership skills. There is no question that virtual and augmented reality will

Opposite: A soldier uses a VR headset in training; the monitor shows the scenario he sees.

change the way that the military prepares for and conducts warfare. Perhaps they already have.

VR AND AR IN THE AIR

In April 2018, the US Air Force launched the Pilot Training Next program to explore the use of virtual reality technology, including headsets, as a way to teach pilots. The air force has a need for more pilots, especially fighter pilots. Therefore, they want to streamline the training process.

This technology is more realistic than ever before. Trainees enter a chamber where they put on a virtual reality headset that transports them to the cockpit of a plane. The sights and sounds mimic those of an actual aircraft, and they hear instructions from the trainers. Students see everything in 360 degrees, as if it were actually present: the controls, display, and battle space. The technology includes biometric sensors that convey information about the students' heart rate and pulse back to instructors. If a student seems to be overwhelmed, indicated by an elevated heart rate or pulse, instructors can make the scenario easier to help the student regain confidence. The immersive quality of the VR experience helps students' brains react as if they were in an actual cockpit. One of the advantages of VR pilot training is that the headsets can be linked so that a group of students can fly their planes together in virtual combat, the way they might in an actual maneuver. In addition to these benefits, this style of training presents

Different civilian and military flight simulators offer varying levels of intensity and immersion. Here, a man manipulates the controls of a civilian flight simulator to guide a plane over virtual terrain.

fewer risks than putting pilots in training in actual cockpits before they're ready.

In the future, the US Air Force hopes to apply the technology to other areas, including medical and aircraft maintenance training.

VR AND AR ON THE GROUND

The first time soldiers find themselves in battle surrounded by gunfire and the chaos of war, they have to make split-second decisions that affect their survival. Traditional training cannot always prepare them for this. The US Army and the US Marine Corps are trying to address this problem by using virtual and augmented reality to give ground troops a more realistic experience of battle. Using virtual and augmented reality to train troops can reduce the risks of training accidents and help soldiers develop the mental, emotional, and physical skills to face combat.

In combat simulations, recruits wear virtual reality goggles or head-mounted displays and body armor that incorporate tracking systems. The displays show the troops images as they move through a virtual 3D environment. In a typical scenario, soldiers might face enemy fire while moving through a hostile region. The system can add challenges such as bad weather. The troops shoot virtual or mock weapons, which act like real weapons. Virtual combat helps reinforce the benefits of following orders and working together, and it provides a sense of what real combat is like.

IST PLATOON
LIVE PARTICIPANT

2ND PLATOON
REMOTE PARTICIPANT

A vehicle commander interacts with a soldier's avatar, or digital image, that is operated remotely during training.

The army's synthetic training environment (STE) is an immersive system. It places soldiers in diverse combat environments in which they experience various demanding scenarios. The training stresses them mentally as well as physically, making them better prepared to face real combat. The system is the result of the joint efforts of the Army Research Laboratory, the University of Southern California Institute for Creative Technologies, and the Combined Arms Center Training and Program Executive Office for Simulation, Training, and Instrumentation.

Together, these three groups are refining the system to better accommodate soldiers' training needs.

Augmented reality can be used in actual combat as well as in training simulations. The US military is exploring the use of AR glasses and displays by ground troops. Wearable glasses and headsets allow key data to be overlaid onto troops' view of the battlefield. These devices can show mapping information as well as markers indicating the movements of both enemy and allied troops. Drones flying overhead can download video showing the activities occurring in remote locations. Because AR glasses are transparent, unlike virtual reality headsets, the wearers can simultaneously see their immediate environment and what's going on remotely. AR headsets give troops a 360-degree view of the battlefield, and the system can use an artificial intelligence (AI) image recognition system to automatically track combatants. Artificial intelligence is programming a computer to complete tasks and activities usually associated with living beings, such as recognizing an image.

This type of technology is being incorporated in combat vehicles as well. The CV90 battle station by BAE Systems is an example of a military vehicle designed to process AR data for use in combat. The CV90 is already a formidable tank-like machine that can hold eight people and shoot multiple sizes of explosive shells. BAE's goal is to create AR-enabled combat vehicles—including tanks, planes, and boats—equipped with sensors and imaging systems so that troops inside can view what's happening outside the vehicle, as if the vehicle were transparent. Among other advantages, this means that the gunner of a tank could operate the weapon from inside the tank without having to expose himself to enemy fire by sticking his head out to aim the weapon.

As mentioned, pilots can train using virtual reality. Interestingly, however, pilots are not the only flight-based personnel who are trained using this technology. Airborne soldiers, who parachute from planes and helicopters into war zones, train with VR technology as well. For example, special operations personnel use a virtual reality trainer to

VR applications can train military personnel to work together on missions.

prepare for their real drops. The trainer lets them rehearse a drop multiple times before they embark on a mission. One system, PARASIM, uses a VR headset and a special harness similar to that on a parachute. The computer-created environment includes simulated weather and map imagery. The system lets a group of airborne soldiers perform as a team, as they would on the actual mission.

There are other technologies that allow soldiers to practice missions as well. Battlefield commanders in charge of small units are the key decision-makers during combat. They must rapidly make life-and-death choices. The US Marine Corps provides groups of soldiers with "tactical decision kits" to help improve these decision-making capabilities. The tactical decision kits were developed by the Marine Corps' Rapid Capabilities Office, whose mission is to rapidly design and develop new technologies. The kits contain the Interactive Tactical Decision Game (I-TDG) with an augmented reality application, a Microsoft HoloLens visual display, and a system that rapidly surveys and models terrain. The kits can be used both with other first-person simulation tools and during actual field exercises.

Using the system, marines can plan missions and conduct "what if" tactical decision exercises. It can digitally record virtual or live exercise scenarios and use them in games that can be shared across a battalion, or a large group of troops. The shared augmented reality environment created by the system lets marines see each other and their surroundings while playing the game.

A MORE ADVANCED MILITARY

The use of advanced technology creates a need for soldiers, sailors, marines, and airmen who are better educated and have the ability to learn high-tech skills. Luckily, as the need for soldiers comfortable with technology has increased, so has the familiarity of recruits with AR, VR, and interactive computer technology. Many recruits already have basic skills in targeting and activating virtual weapons because of extensive use of flight simulators and first-person shooter technology in video games. In addition, experience with war games has taught recruits to make decisions regarding the approach to battle and to work as a member of a team in combat.

Some recruits are more prepared to train using VR and AR applications because they've already used similar gaming technologies.

A second way in which AR and VR, as well as other advanced computer technologies, have affected military recruitment is that they have created a need for college-educated science and technology majors. Software developers, programmers, computer technicians, and equipment engineers are needed to create the next-generation AR and VR systems that will be used in both training and battle.

VR AND AR AT SEA

Like the air force, the navy has long employed simulators to train pilots of sea-based vehicles such as submarines. Some simulators are static (nonmoving), showing changes in instrument readings that trainees must address, allowing them to learn how to respond to emergencies. Other simulators use mechanical systems like hydraulics, which use liquid and pressure to make things move, to mimic the pitch and roll of a real submarine as it descends and rises.

For surface ships, there is a simulator that recreates the actions that occur on a ship's bridge, where the ship's controls are located. To replicate the ship's environment, display monitors are used as the bridge's windows. The simulator teaches ship-handling techniques, such as steering and navigation. In addition, trainees learn how to work together as a team in different situations.

The Office of Naval Research (ONR) supports the use of virtual reality applications for training purposes. For example, the Fleet Integrated Synthetic Training/Testing Facility (FIST2FAC) has been given the responsibility for designing, developing, testing, and demonstrating simulator-based training technologies that combine virtual elements with live-action exercises. According to Dr. Terry Allard, head of the Warfighter Performance Department at ONR, "This is the future of training for the Navy. With simulation, you can explore endless possibilities without the expense and logistical challenges of putting hundreds of ships at sea and aircraft in the sky."

Full bodysuits can be used to track a person's movements to create a 3D avatar. Here, a virtual puppeteer (the man in black) prepares to interact with marines during a training exercise developed by the Office of Naval Research.

FIST2FAC combines software and gaming technology to put sailors in various virtual settings. The technology can create scenarios that incorporate vehicles such as aircraft carriers and helicopters, as well as both lethal and nonlethal weapons. In one example, sailors at Ford Island, Hawaii, manned a virtual ship that was being attacked by a swarm of small, fast boats. Using virtual training environments is significantly less expensive than training in a physical environment with real ships and aircraft.

Virtual training provides other advantages as well. It allows sailors to be trained in the specific environments in which they will be deployed. The ONR has developed and tested a variety of simulation tools for use on land and sea. One example is the Battlespace Exploitation of Mixed Reality system, which uses a combination of virtual reality and augmented reality. For instance, the technology can superimpose virtual element on the users' real environment. Prior to deployment, users can immerse themselves in the environment they will be fighting in so that they are prepared.

The US Navy hasn't restricted its use of virtual reality to training, however. It has pioneered a virtual reality recruitment tool to attract cadets to the naval academy. It is a video game system housed in a tractor trailer truck, which allows it to be moved to different recruitment sites. The tractor trailer truck travels around the country to special events and schools to find students in STEM (science, technology, engineering, and math) programs. It contains eight VR pods, which collectively can hold about sixty people. The simulation employs the Oculus Rift VR system to provide an experience of being in the navy. In one example, players are on a mission to rescue a Navy SEAL team. The team of players must navigate a waterway, fire guns, and launch grenades to save the SEAL team, while under fire. The navy has been able to gain commitments from twice as many potential recruits using the game than with other recruitment methods.

3 MILITARY CAREERS

Before you prepare for a career as a programmer in the military, you need to consider whether the military is the right environment for you. As a programmer, whether in VR and AR or in areas such as cybersecurity, you are unlikely to be on the front lines in combat. Nonetheless, working in the military is different from being employed in a civilian job. It offers the satisfaction of doing something challenging and meaningful and can provide funds for college or graduate school. If you join a branch of the service, it will pay all or part of any student loans you have acquired in the course of pursuing your education.

Opposite: Computer programmers and software engineers work in teams on both domestic and foreign bases like this one in the United Arab Emirates.

Also, once you complete your enlistment, you are eligible for veterans' benefits, including health care and further education assistance. However, life in the military is a more regulated and restricted lifestyle than civilian life. You have no control over where you are sent to work. Even if you are an officer, there will always be someone of a higher rank giving you orders, which you must follow. You do not have the option of quitting if you don't like your boss or your orders until your contract is complete or you are released from service. If you do decide that the military is the right work environment for you, there are a number of options for a programming career.

ENLISTING IN THE MILITARY

There are two levels of personnel in the military. There are enlisted personnel and officers. To enlist in the military, you must be at least eighteen—or seventeen with parental consent. Recruits must have at least a high school diploma or General Educational Development (GED) certificate, indicating that they have met high school equivalency requirements. They must be US citizens or permanent legal residents of the United States and must meet physical fitness requirements. Additionally, the military will not accept a recruit with a criminal record for serious crimes.

All recruits also must take the Armed Services Vocational Aptitude Battery (ASVAB) test. The ASVAB is much like the SAT or ACT tests you take before applying to college. It covers the following:

- arithmetic reasoning
- mathematics knowledge
- word knowledge
- paragraph comprehension
- assembling objects
- auto information
- shop information
- electronics information
- general science
- mechanical comprehension

The score on the test determines for which careers a recruit is eligible. Achieving a high score requires a good knowledge of math, science, and—for computer science—electronics information. Recruits with at least twenty semester hours of college and those who have completed three years in a high school Junior Reserve Officers' Training Corps (JROTC) program can enter the military at a higher rank. Most college graduates in computer science or programming qualify for officer training and enter the military as an officer.

The military branches also offer ROTC programs at colleges and universities around the United States. They provide scholarships to high school and college students who qualify academically. The scholarships consist of partial or full tuition and a nontaxable monthly stipend. Some colleges provide ROTC students with additional financial aid for tuition, fees, and books.

In the army, a job held by an enlisted soldier is referred to as an MOS, or Military Occupational Specialty. The army is the only branch of the service that offers a guaranteed job (MOS) to everyone. Which MOSs are offered to a recruit depends upon his or her qualifications and what jobs have current or projected openings.

In the air force, jobs for enlisted personnel are Air Force Specialty Codes (AFSCs). The air force provides both Guaranteed Job and Guaranteed Aptitude Area programs. In the Guaranteed Job program, the applicant is guaranteed a specific job. In the Guaranteed Aptitude Area program, the applicant is guaranteed that he or she will be placed in a job that falls into one of four aptitude areas: general, electronic, mechanical, or administrative. If you are denied the guaranteed job in your contract because of something beyond your control (such as the elimination of the job), you will have the option of choosing a new job or asking for a discharge, which means being released from your military contract.

Those who enlist as soldiers, sailors, or airmen might participate in some training that involves virtual reality or might have the opportunity to use it as part of a research project or in the field. However, most of their time will not be spent using virtual reality. The exceptions are software programmers, some of whom might be assigned to work on virtual reality projects, and people who eventually become trainers who work with virtual reality training equipment. Most computer programming positions require a college degree. However, it is possible to enter the military as

In addition to an aptitude test, soldiers undergo basic training in which they have to test their skills and physical abilities. For instance, this recruit is participating in a land navigation exercise.

a computer programming specialist directly out of high school. For example, the air force has a program for high school graduates who:

- are between ages seventeen and thirty-nine;
- have a high school diploma, or GED with fifteen college credits;
- complete a Computer Systems Programming Initial Skills course;
- attain a score of at least seventy-one on the Air Force Electronic Data Processing Test;
- successfully pass a background check; and
- complete Basic Military Training as well as Airmen's Week.

ENTERING THE MILITARY AS AN OFFICER

If you obtain a four-year college degree, for instance in computer science, you can enter the military as an officer. You can enroll in Officer Candidate School (OCS), which is also called Officer Training School (OTS) in the US Air Force. Officer training generally lasts nine to seventeen weeks, depending on the service. Classes cover military subjects, physical training, and leadership skills. If the service has a need for individuals with specific skills, it sometimes directly commissions candidates. These recruits attend Officer Indoctrination School (OIS), Officer Development School (ODS), or the Direct Commission

WAR GAMES

There has long been a symbiotic, or mutually beneficial, relationship between the military and the computer gaming industry. The military provides funding and technical assistance to game developers. In exchange, the game manufacturers provide the military with exclusive technology and consulting services. The military encourages its soldiers to play computer war games as a way to maintain combat training and stay in a military mindset when not on active duty. Games such as *UrbanSim* and *Frontlines: Fuel of War* teach players other aspects of modern warfare. Players battle militants, deal with uprisings and counterattacks, experience the dangers of explosive devices, and learn the usefulness of weaponized drones.

Computer games don't really capture the nature of a soldier's life, however. Real service consists of more than battles. Most soldiers never even experience large battlefield operations. Additionally, in the digital world there are no lasting physical, legal, or ethical consequences. If you die in a game, you just start another one. If you kill virtual combatants or innocent bystanders, there are no emotional scars. When soldiers actually shoot people, it has a powerful emotional effect that games do not prepare them for. Thus, video games improve soldiers' physical skills, such as eye-hand coordination, but they do not fully prepare soldiers for the trauma of real combat.

Officer Indoctrination Course (DCOIC), depending on which branch of the military they join. Another option is to join the Reserve Officers' Training Corps (ROTC). This program covers all or part of a student's tuition in college in return for a commitment to join one of the branches of the service as an officer upon graduation.

An example of a direct commission officer (DCO) program is the army's Cyber Direct Commissioning Program, which recruits civilians to become officers in the army and the US Army National Guard. Those recruits develop programs and devices that assist soldiers in operating in cyberspace. The program is run by the US Army Cyber Command. Army cyber officers use their civilian education and experience to write programs and to conduct research in their area of computer expertise.

Those who qualify for the Cyber Direct Commissioning Program attend two army schools: a six-week Direct Commissioning Course and the twelve-week Cyber Basic Officer Leader Course. After completing these courses, they might qualify for additional training not available in the civilian sector. To qualify for the program, one must be a US citizen, have at least a four-year college degree, meet the army's physical fitness requirement, and be eligible for a top-secret security clearance. Army cyber officers must commit to serving for three years. They enter the army with the rank of first lieutenant or higher, depending on their level of education and expertise.

Cadets graduating from West Point, the army's military academy, enter the service as officers.

MILITARY COMPUTER SOFTWARE DEVELOPER

Level:	Varies
Years of Experience Required:	Varies
Education Needed:	Bachelor's degree or higher
Specific Requirements:	Knowledge of one or more of computer languages such as C, C++, Python, Java, CUDA, OpenCL, Linux; experience developing software for VR/AR applications, including 2D and 3D graphics; knowledge of project development procedures; self-starter with strong interpersonal communications skills and ability to work with geographically diverse groups; security clearance

Programming jobs in the military are similar to those in the private sector, except that the material you'd work with in the military may be classified. This means that you must be able to qualify for a security clearance. To qualify for one, you must have a clean criminal record and pass a drug test.

The responsibilities of a VR/AR software developer include writing VR/AR programs for military aviation, ground vehicles, weapon systems, or training simulators,

The military contracts civilian companies for some of its programming needs. Here, software developers work together to create and deliver a military application.

as part of a research or development team. Software developers also test and document their programs.

The salary that a person makes in the military depends on his or her assigned pay grade, which is determined by his or her job, rank, years of experience, education, and years in the military. Salaries in the military are generally lower than those in civilian life. However, the military pays for, or gives additional cash allowances for, many expenses not covered by civilian employers. Therefore, when you take total compensation into consideration, the salaries are comparable.

For example, pay for a college-educated software developer who is an officer would be in the $75,000–$100,000 range. Civilian pay for such positions is likely to be $15,000–$20,000 higher. However, the military personnel receive an annual food allowance of about $3,000–$4,000 for a single person, a housing allowance of over $10,000, and free health care, so they have no health insurance costs. Companies do not pay for food and housing, and usually employees pay at least part of their health insurance costs. Therefore, total compensation is often similar, despite the fact that the listed salary is lower in the military than in the civilian sector. Additionally, the military will pay for educational expenses, either in preparation for a military career, via an ROTC program; during service at one of the military-run schools or a civilian college or university; or after service, through the GI Bill, which provides veterans with funds for further education.

VR/AR TRAINER

Level:	Experienced
Years of Experience Required:	Five years instructor or training experience
Education Needed:	High school diploma or GED
Specific Requirements:	Preferably a graduate of either the US Army Combined Arms and Services Staff School (CAS3), Officer or Warrant Officer Advanced Course, Primary or Advanced Non-Commissioned Officers Course; experience with providing instruction for tactical operation of platoons, companies and troops, and their support units

Not all VR and AR jobs in the military are dedicated software development positions. There are also VR/AR-related jobs as a computer-based training specialist/instructor (CBTI). The responsibilities of this type of

A trainer uses a microphone to communicate with trainees in a simulator.

position include instructing trainees as they use simulators and creating scenarios to encourage trainees to master tactical skills. This requires controlling manned simulators and teaching trainees how to handle different aspects of battle. This type of job may also require you to use specialized software, programming tools, and hardware to write and edit instructional text, audio, graphics, and video for interactive experiences. This portion of the job may be done in conjunction with a development team. Since you'd have specialized knowledge of the trainees' needs, you'd be able to communicate them to developers, so collaborative skills would also be important to this role.

As you can see from these examples, the best way to qualify for a VR/AR career in the military is to get a college degree with a special focus in that area. It remains important, however, to gain experience working for companies in that field while you are in school, over the summer, or after graduating.

4 PREPARATION FOR THESE CAREERS

Virtual and augmented reality programmers need strong technical skills, including knowledge of computer languages and software tools that are used to create VR and AR applications. They also need a knowledge of the physics and engineering principles that govern how computers work and the way vehicles and equipment perform. The latter is beneficial because the VR and AR applications created will need to make virtual objects behave in ways that mimic the operation of their counterparts in the real world. There is no way to know exactly what type of project you will work on. You might have to create software that analyzes data from sensors on unmanned drones to create real-time

Opposite: Students can learn basic programming skills in middle and high school.

displays, or you may have to develop training simulations that reproduce combat situations. Thus, it is vital to learn the basic skills that can be applied to a variety of projects. In addition, a strong foundation will make it easier to learn new programming languages and tools.

PREPARING IN HIGH SCHOOL

Aspiring VR and AR programmers should study math and physics in high school because they need to understand the physics that govern the way machines and objects behave

Students need to develop strong interpersonal skills for VR and AR jobs in the military.

in the real world. Similarly, math is required to create computer algorithms, which are sets of rules computers follow. Also, a branch of mathematics called calculus, which is taught in college and some high schools, is needed for physics. To prepare for advanced mathematics courses in college, you should take classes in algebra and precalculus in high school—and calculus, if your school offers it. VR and AR simulations respond to users by calculating the odds of various outcomes of users' actions, so learning statistics and probability is important as well.

There are other skills outside of math and science that are important. On the job, you will need to communicate effectively with team members and write software documentation and reports. Therefore, you must learn proper English grammar and syntax (the rules that govern how words are used in sentences). Programmers spend the bulk of their time at a keyboard, so taking a typing or keyboarding course can make you more efficient.

BEING A LEADER

Although gaining technical skills is incredibly important, working with VR and AR in the military requires personal skills as well. Everything in the military is done as part of a team. Leadership skills are extremely important for those who want to succeed in the military, receive promotions to senior positions, and lead projects.

A leader can motivate people to perform the actions necessary to reach a goal, can organize people and resources

Students need to learn to take the lead when working in collaborative environments. Being a captain of a sports team or stepping up in group projects provides great leadership experience and builds confidence.

effectively, and can keep others working toward a goal, even when obstacles arise. To be a leader, you must be able to communicate clearly and effectively in order to explain the objective and the steps necessary to achieve it.

Above all, leaders must have personal qualities that make other people respect and follow them. Among the most important qualities are the following:

- Self-discipline: This is the ability to carry out the work that must be done, even when no one is forcing you to do it.
- Organizational ability: You must be able to break tasks down into steps that will accomplish a goal. This involves prioritizing tasks and making a schedule indicating what needs to be done, by whom, and by what date.
- Empathy: This is the ability to put yourself in someone else's place and understand a situation as he or she does. Having empathy allows you to encourage, reassure, and instruct others effectively.
- Dependability: Dependability, or trustworthiness, means standing by your word and doing what you say you will.

Demonstrating good leadership skills will make you a more desirable candidate for the military. It will also make you more successful in your career. You can develop leadership skills by participating in school fundraising projects such as car washes, school clubs, political campaigns, social action groups, neighborhood projects such as playground cleanups, and charity events such as races.

EDUCATION FOR SOFTWARE DEVELOPMENT

Most software developer jobs require a four-year college degree. For more advanced positions, a master's degree or PhD is desirable. The level of education is one factor that determines the rank at which a person will enter the military. Students working toward a degree in software development will study both software and hardware, meaning the programs as well as the equipment used to run them. They must understand the principles of how the equipment works in order to create effective software. Besides learning various programming languages and software creation tools, students are taught how to work on projects and solve problems. Colleges and universities offer bachelor's, master's, and PhD degrees. Technical institutes provide both two-year associate's degree programs and four-year degree programs.

Another option is to study for a degree online. Software development lends itself to this approach because programming can be done easily at home. However, one must have a great deal of self-discipline to do the work without the support system provided by a physical college. If you decide to study online, make sure that you enroll

DEVELOPING YOUR PROGRAMMING SKILLS IN HIGH SCHOOL

Gaining programming experience makes you better prepared for college courses. There are many ways to develop computing and programming skills. There are books and free or fee-based courses that offer training for beginners in creating virtual reality apps. Among these are a number of tutorials available for the Unreal Engine and Unity game engines. These are platforms with which you can literally build virtual reality games. Both platforms offer instructional support and courses.

Another way to learn about programming and about virtual and augmented reality is to join a professional organization. Two major computing industry organizations are the Institute of Electrical and Electronics Engineers (IEEE) and the Association for Computing Machinery (ACM). These organizations both offer memberships and provide special resources for students. Joining and participating in such organizations provides students with knowledge of what it is like to be a software programmer and the issues they face. It also gives students a chance to make contacts with professionals to whom they can turn for advice.

in a bachelor's degree program in software development. Simply taking a multiweek online course in creating virtual reality apps will not give you the kind of education that a programming position in the military requires. In addition, make sure that the software development program offered by the online university includes courses in VR and AR.

Most important, make sure that the institution offering the program is accredited. Accreditation guarantees that the degree you receive is valid and that the credits you receive for courses are transferrable to another school if you decide to switch to a different university. Check the US Department of Education's Database of Accredited Postsecondary Institutions and Programs to determine a prospective university's status (https://ope.ed.gov/dapip).

SOFTWARE DEVELOPMENT CURRICULUM

Only a few colleges and universities offer degree programs specifically in virtual and augmented reality. Instead, aspiring VR and AR developers can enter a general software developer degree program and learn all the techniques required to be a programmer. In addition, they can take courses in specialized areas of programming, such as VR and AR. The exact courses that programming students take vary from school to school. However, the following material provides a general idea of the coursework required.

Students take general courses in computer science, mathematics, and the natural sciences. The computer science courses cover general principles and a variety

In college, students have the opportunity to interact with experts in the field. You should never hesitate to ask questions or ask for further guidance.

of programming languages, which can be applied to any specialty students later undertake. In addition, students take courses in specific areas of computer science such as VR and AR. Many college VR courses focus on gaming, animation, or film production. Knowledge of such areas can be beneficial for later creating scenarios or "war games" for training simulations. Courses in artificial intelligence are also helpful, as military and other simulation VR programs require computers to use AI to respond to users' actions. Students usually take mathematics courses such as advanced forms of calculus and algebra, as well as probability and statistics.

Courses in physics, basic engineering principles, and experimental design are also part of the curriculum. These are particularly important for VR programming. A programmer must understand the principles that govern the behavior of machines and equipment in order to create virtual versions that operate as they do in real life.

These more obvious courses often aren't the only ones students will take. Some schools may also require students to take a course in ethical computing, which covers topics such as how to maintain the confidentiality of data and protect people's privacy. Additionally, a software developer needs good communication and managerial skills. When someone works as part of a project team, organizational and people skills are critical to a project's success. This is especially true in the military, where people may be assigned to a project from a pool of qualified personnel. A person must be able to work and communicate with people of varied backgrounds and skills. Many college software development programs include a course on communications for engineers. It is highly recommended that you take such a course if the school provides it, even if it isn't specifically required. The same applies to taking a project management course, especially if you are earning a higher degree. It is quite likely that at some point you will be expected to run a project, and doing so successfully will be critical for your career in the military.

As part of a bachelor's degree program, students take a variety of courses in the humanities and arts, in addition to their technical classes. For a military career, courses in history, psychology, and languages are particularly beneficial. Not only are military personnel sometimes stationed overseas, but they come from many different ethnic and racial backgrounds. A knowledge of other cultures and languages can help you understand others and make working with a diverse group easier.

College is the time to develop good work habits. In software development, you will often have to complete your part of a project on time without supervision and generate high-quality work. If you develop these habits in high school and college, you will improve your chances of being successful in the military.

THE ROTC OPTION

College is expensive. For those interested in a programming career in the military, one option to make college more affordable is to enter the Reserve Officers' Training Corps (ROTC) program. This program, which is offered at more than 1,700 colleges and universities throughout the United States, provides students with scholarships for college in return for an agreement to become officers in the US military. Each branch of the service has its own ROTC program. The ROTC academic curriculum for those choosing a Marine Corps option includes classes in national security policy and the history of American military affairs, in addition to the regular ROTC academic requirements.

In the ROTC programs, students learn leadership development and military skills and receive career training. Participants take both classroom and field training in addition to their regular academic studies. They can also participate in additional summer programs. After completing the program and graduating, students are given officer status in the army, navy, marines, or air force.

CONTINUED LEARNING

If you pursue a career in VR and AR, you will be in a field where the technology changes rapidly and continuously. New devices and computing technologies will be invented, and military personnel will need to be trained in their use. Therefore, software developers and people serving in the armed forces must be prepared to continue learning throughout their careers. Many civilian and military colleges offer courses that allow software developers to stay current with the latest technologies. In some cases, it is also possible for military programmers with a bachelor's degree to have their courses for a more advanced degree paid for by the military.

In addition to college-level ROTC programs, Junior ROTC programs allow students to train and develop leadership skills while they are still in high school.

REALITY POSTER
SOLAR SYSTEM
Galaxy
Jupiter
Uranus
Nebula
Star Cluster
Mars
Jupiter
Venus
Sun
Mercury
Earth
Neptune
Saturn
Pluto
Black Hole
Full
Moon Phases
TAP ME
TAP ME
TAP ME
TAP ME
APP!

5 FUTURE TECH

The applications for VR and AR are advancing rapidly in many fields, and the military is no exception. All the branches of service are exploring new ways to employ these technologies both in the field and remotely.

ENHANCING NAVAL READINESS

Section 219 of the National Defense Authorization Act allows warfare centers and research laboratories to engage in partnerships with industry and academic organizations to pursue research, engineering, and technology development projects. This has spurred the

Opposite: Here, an airman engages with an AR map of the solar system, providing an interactive learning experience.

US Navy to work with private companies on researching AR and VR technology.

As part of the navy's program, the Naval Surface Warfare Center, Port Hueneme Division (NSWC PHD) has partnered with a company called Moback to investigate the use of specialized AR and VR capabilities. Moback develops cloud-based AR applications, including AR animations that can be viewed on a mobile device. Together, the navy and the company are investigating the application of the technology to naval training, maintenance, and engineering. One such application is fixing or upgrading shipboard equipment and combat weapons remotely. In 2018, the commanding officer of the NSWC PHD, Captain Ray Acevedo, said, "Working on AR and VR capabilities is critical to our fleet support mission and will allow us to significantly increase the lethal capabilities of our Navy."

NEW WAYS OF SEEING

In 2018, Samsung and Sony were attempting to replace heads-up displays with much tinier displays—AR contact lenses. Samsung wanted to develop them as an accessory to smartphones. Sony wanted to develop them as general AR devices. In the same year, weapons manufacturer BAE Systems announced that it would introduce these types of contact lenses to provide portable command centers to help soldiers identify threats and target them. Even more advanced displays are being explored by manufacturers. Among these are virtual retinal displays (VRDs), which

Some companies are developing AR contact lenses. In the military, these could provide soldiers with more information without a lot of equipment.

would create images by projecting light from a laser into the human eye. In 2018, however, this type of technology was still in the very early stages of development. That said, this isn't the only type of cutting edge innovation out there.

The US Air Force's 412th Electronic Warfare Group also started exploring AR technology as a means to make the invisible visible. They believe the technology could be used to show aircraft pilots virtual electronic signals from antennae and virtual images of the effects of electromagnetic interference, or interference from radio frequencies.

Researchers also believe that AR systems could eventually be loaded with 3D renderings of internal aircraft structures. This would let maintenance personnel see virtual drawings of the wiring, hydraulic, and fuel systems of aircraft while they work. The US Air Force has explored this as a possible means of eliminating printed maintenance instructions. It is even researching the possibility of projecting AR images directly on the equipment being worked on, showing what needs to be done.

HEALING THE TRAUMA OF WAR

In addition to training military personnel, VR and AR technology has the potential to help veterans recover from the trauma of war. These technologies are being explored for use in treating post-traumatic stress disorder (PTSD) in soldiers. PTSD is a disorder caused by psychologically intense experiences. Sufferers struggle with sleeplessness, depression, difficulty concentrating, vivid memories of the traumatic event(s), and other effects. Many individuals who have fought in wars suffer from this disorder.

To treat PTSD using VR, therapists will immerse veterans in VR scenarios that mirror their wartime experiences. This gives veterans the opportunity to safely confront their experiences. For instance, Pandemic Studio's video game *Full Spectrum Warrior* is being adapted by researchers for use in a virtual exposure treatment. The idea is that repeat exposure will lessen the impact and anxiety related to the event. The game can be used to create customized scenarios that address specific battlefield traumas.

VIDEO GAMES AND DRONES

Operating VR-enabled systems is more familiar to younger members of the military, who grew up playing the latest video games. At a meeting of the Association for Unmanned Vehicle Systems International (AUVSI), board of directors member Tim Owings discussed the increasing use of unmanned aerial vehicles (UAVs) in the military. He also described the success the US Army has had using teenagers as operators of UAVs. The controls of the remote vehicle systems are similar to video game controls. Because of the teenagers' experience playing video games, they demonstrate great proficiency at operating remote vehicles.

People's experiences operating video game controls makes them adept at controlling drones.

Video games are beneficial in more ways than one. Research has shown that playing video games can train users to process audiovisual information faster. It can also help them to interpret multiple sources of information simultaneously. As augmented reality becomes a more significant part of the operation of unmanned vehicles, teenagers' expertise in playing VR and AR games will no doubt be another valuable skill.

A military therapist uses Virtual Iraq VR therapy to help a soldier with PSTD.

Dr. Skip Rizzo, the director of the University of Southern California's Medical Virtual Reality Lab, designs simulations of military settings in Afghanistan and Iraq for this purpose. According to Rizzo, "We put them in a world most similar to the kind of experiences that they had when they were in combat, in their traumatic moments."

For instance, Rizzo went on, simulations may place users "where they saw a person die, or [where] they killed someone or got blown up in a vehicle." Being re-exposed to the situation gives soldiers a chance to address and come to terms with their feelings about the experience.

THE TOLL OF VIRTUAL REALITY

The use of VR and AR in combat is not without drawbacks. There are practical problems with relying on VR and AR systems in war. Computers could malfunction, leaving data-dependent soldiers vulnerable. Worse, they could be hacked, and troops could be supplied with misinformation.

Another issue is the psychological toll. On one hand, having data right before one's eyes, such as terrain information and markers of enemy locations, could relieve some of the stress of the decision-making a soldier has to do on the fly. On the other hand, having too much constantly changing information and too many notifications and alerts on AR gear could be both distracting and stressful.

The adoption of VR and AR technology, and the advances in remote-controlled weaponized drones, create new possibilities for the ways in which we fight future warfare. Wars could be waged by drones operated remotely by military personnel immersed in virtual reality environments. Conducting war remotely and killing real people can have serious negative effects on the mental health of operators. This is especially true if civilians are accidently killed. Beyond this, the ability to kill remotely

Motion sickness, like the nausea and headaches some people experience when riding in cars or on trains, is a risk related to VR and AR usage that could be dangerous for military personnel in combat.

leads to dehumanization of the people in the country being attacked. It may be too much like a video game after all, in which one can kill with no chance of being injured. And this killing without consequences can carry over to an increase in violent tendencies upon return to civilian life.

THE FUTURE

As can be seen from these examples, VR and AR are likely to become increasingly important for many types of applications in the military. A wide variety of interesting programs and systems are being created. For that reason, the number of software developers involved in such projects is likely to grow over time, both in the military and at companies that contract with the military to provide VR and AR applications. Therefore, young people who are interested in a computer career in the military should explore it. It is necessary to keep in mind, however, that there is no guarantee which area of computer science a programmer might be assigned to, unless this is arranged in advance. Pursuing a general computer science education might lead to you being assigned to something other than VR work, such as cybersecurity. If you want to be assigned work in virtual and augmented reality, you should make sure to study VR and AR as much as possible.

GLOSSARY

accreditation The process of ensuring that an educational institution has met the requirements to provide degrees.

artificial intelligence (AI) Programming a computer to complete tasks and activities usually associated with living beings, such as recognizing an image.

augmented reality (AR) A technology that places computer-generated images in a user's real-world field of vision through devices like smartphones, smart glasses, or heads-up displays.

depth tracking The tracking of the distance of an object and the supplying of that information to a computer system.

global positioning system (GPS) A satellite-based system that supplies location information to computers in vehicles and other devices.

heads-up display A transparent display on which the user can view computer-generated information while still seeing the real world.

hydraulic Mechanically operated by pressure created from the movement of liquid.

immersive A 3D experience a user can be totally submerged in.

peripheral vision The ability to see what is on the side without a person rotating his or her eyes or turning his or her head.

pitch and roll The up-and-down and side-to-side movement, respectively, of a ship or plane.

post-traumatic stress disorder (PTSD) A syndrome caused by a psychologically intense experience, which causes sleeplessness, depression, difficulty concentrating, vivid memories of the event, and other effects; many people who have fought in wars suffer from it.

probability The analysis of how likely various events are to occur.

rendering A 3D drawing that serves as an outline or a blueprint.

retina The cells in the back of the eye that receive light-related data.

rudder A movable mechanical device used to stabilize an aircraft or boat.

simultaneous localization and mapping (SLAM) The process of creating a map using a robot or unmanned vehicle that navigates that environment.

superimpose To place one image over another so that both can be seen at the same time.

symbiotic The interaction of two things in which the interaction is mutually beneficial.

vestibular system The parts of the ear and associated nerves that transmit information to the brain about a human body's orientation in the environment.

virtual reality (VR) An immersive, computer-generated, 3D simulation that places a user in a digital environment through the use of special hardware like helmets and gloves.

FURTHER INFORMATION

Books

Allen, Robertson. *America's Digital Army: Games at Work and War.* Anthropology of Contemporary North America. Lincoln: University of Nebraska Press, 2017.

Gregory, Josh. *21st Century Skills Innovation Library: Virtual Reality.* Ann Arbor, MI: Cherry Lake Publishing, 2017.

Henneberg, Susan. *Virtual Reality.* Opposing Viewpoints. New York: Greenhaven Press, 2017.

Martin, Brett S. *Virtual Reality.* Tech Bytes: High Tech. Chicago: Norwood House Press, 2017.

Mealy, Paul. *Virtual and Augmented Reality for Dummies.* Hoboken, NJ: John Wiley, 2018.

Websites

Junior Reserve Officers' Training Corps (JROTC)

http://www.usarmyjrotc.com

The JROTC website contains information on joining this military training program while in high school.

Makezine: Getting Started with VR

https://makezine.com/2016/03/24/makers-introduction-vr-best-software-tools-free

This article provides a list of free VR platforms and software tools that can be used to make VR apps.

Today's Military: ROTC Programs

https://www.todaysmilitary.com/training/rotc

This website provides information on all aspects of the ROTC program, including links to the programs in all the different branches of the military.

US Army Cyber Command

https://www.arcyber.army.mil

The US Army Cyber Command website provides information on the various computer-related careers in the army and their requirements.

Videos

SimX: VR Military Medical Training Simulation

https://www.youtube.com/watch?v=2RYQeSxPWa0

This video shows a brief case on the SimX VR medical simulation system designed for military medics.

Tactical Augmented Reality

https://www.youtube.com/watch?v=x8p19j8C6VI

This video displays how the US Army hopes to use AR technology in combat.

SELECTED BIBLIOGRAPHY

"Augmented Reality and Virtual Reality to Enhance
    US Military Training." *ARPost*, December 18, 2017.
    https://arpost.co/2017/12/18/augmented-reality-
    virtual-reality-military-training.

Dubravac, Shawn. *Digital Destiny: How the New Age
    of Data Will Transform the Way We Work, Live,
    and Communicate*. Washington, DC: Regnery
    Publishing, 2015.

Jenkins, Aric. "The Navy Has a New Recruitment
    Tactic: Virtual Reality." *Fortune*, May 30, 2017.
    http://fortune.com/2017/05/30/navy-virtual-
    reality-recruitment.

Losey, Stephen. "The Air Force Is Revolutionizing the
    Way Airmen Learn to Be Aviators." *Air Force Times*,
    September 30, 2018. https://www.airforcetimes.com/
    news/your-air-force/2018/09/30/the-air-force-is-
    revolutionizing-the-way-airmen-learn-to-be-aviators.

Lynch, Gerald. "AR Warfare: How the Military Is Using Augmented Reality." *Tech Radar*, September 16, 2017. https://www.techradar.com/news/death-becomes-ar-how-the-military-is-using-augmented-reality.

McCraine, Samantha, and Max Honigmann. "War Games: Virtual Reality's Bloody New Frontier." *Graphite Publications*, July 16, 2016. https://graphitepublications.com/war-games.

Miller, Susan. "AF Sees Aircraft Maintenance Via Augmented Reality." *Defense Systems*, June 21, 2018. https://defensesystems.com/articles/2018/06/21/af-augmented-reality-aircraft-maintenance.aspx.

Nye, Logan. "The US Military Is Using VR to Simulate
    Combat Jumps." *Business Insider*, May 19, 2017.
    https://www.businessinsider.com/us-military-
    using-new-virtual-reality-trainer-simulate-combat-
    jumps-2017-5.

Office of Naval Research. "Virtual Victories: Marines
    Sharpen Skills with New Virtual-Reality Games."
    Phys.org, May 17, 2017. https://phys.org/news/2017-
    05-virtual-victories-marines-sharpen-skills.html.

Romaniuk, Scott Nicholas, and Tobias Burgers.
    "How the US Military Is Using 'Violent, Chaotic,
    Beautiful' Video Games to Train Soldiers."
    Conversation, March 7, 2017. http://theconversation.
    com/how-the-us-military-is-using-violent-chaotic-
    beautiful-video-games-to-train-soldiers-73826.

Shaban, Hamza. "Playing War: How the Military Uses Video Games." *Atlantic*, October 10, 2013. https://www.theatlantic.com/technology/archive/2013/10/playing-war-how-the-military-uses-video-games/280486.

Seidel, Robert J., and Paul R. Chatelier, eds. *Virtual Reality, Training's Future?: Perspectives on Virtual Reality and Related Emerging Technologies*. Defense Research Series, vol. 6. New York: Plenum Press, 1997.

INDEX

ABOUT THE AUTHOR

Jeri Freedman has a bachelor of arts degree from Harvard University. For fifteen years, she worked for companies involved in cutting-edge technologies, including advanced semiconductors and scientific testing equipment. She was the cofounder of Innovative Applications, a small computer company selling and customizing accounting software. She is the author of more than fifty books, including *Digital Career Building Through Skinning and Modding, Careers in Computer Support, High-Tech Jobs: Software Development, Cyber Citizenship and Cyber Safety: Intellectual Property,* and *Call of Duty, Careers in the Military: Your Career in the Air Force.*